Declare His Name

Declare His Name

A SELECTION OF MISSIONARY HERO SKETCHES, DRAMATIC READINGS, AND DRAMAS FOR ADULTS AND CHILDREN

COMPILED BY

JEANNIE LOCKERBIE STEPHENSON

Association of Baptists for World Evangelism
P.O. Box 8585
Harrisburg, PA 17105–8585
(717) 774–7000
abwe@abwe.org

ABWE Canada
160 Adelaide St. South, Suite 205
London, Ontario N5Z 3L1
(519) 690–1009
office@abwecanada.org

 PUBLISHING®

DECLARE HIS NAME
Copyright © 2001 by ABWE Publishing
Harrisburg, Pennsylvania 17105

Library of Congress Cataloging-in-Publication Data
(Application Pending)

Compiled by Jeannie Lockerbie Stephenson
Lockerbie, Jeannie, 1938–

Declare His Name
  Missions, Non-fiction
  ISBN 1-888796-26-X

Printed in the United States of America.

TABLE OF
CONTENTS

SKETCHES
OF
MISSIONARY
HEROES

by Dr. Jerry Franz

These missionary skits each require three persons. The skits may be performed as a reader's theater, that is, each person reading his part with good interpretation.

or

Presenters may memorize their parts and move around the stage according to the scene portrayed.

Some italicized notes in the parts are more directly applicable if acted on stage, but may also be helpful as interpretation for a reader's theater. The parts designated by the numbers 1, 2, or 3, denote the three actors.

Background information for an in-depth study of the missionary's life is given in the recommended reading section following each skit.

Dr. Jerry Franz is the librarian and associate professor of history at Practical Bible College in Binghamton, N.Y.

BARTHOLOMEW ZIEGENBALG

(all heads bowed, then up together with first line)

1: Missions!

2: Bartholomew Ziegenbalg, a German pietist, went to the southern coast of India in 1706.

3: The first non-Catholic missionary to reach India from Europe.

1: He was twenty-three years old. His motto: Pray and work!

2: Passage from Europe to India took almost eight months.

3: When he arrived, the governor immediately imprisoned him for four months.

2: Leave this place! You will do no good here. No one wants you here. *(governor points and shouts at #1)*

1: "Pray and work."

3: The educated class of society despised him, because he sought to minister to the lower classes. *(actor speaks as an educated person, looking down upon #1 and shaking his head)*

1: "Pray and work."

2: The lower classes seemed uninterested. *(actor speaks in apathetic, uninterested manner)*

1: "Pray and work."

3: Catholic missionaries did all they could to hinder him.

2: This man—do not listen to him! He means you harm! *(#2 shouts to imaginary crowd and points to #1)*

1: "Pray and work."

2: Brahman priests sought to kill him. *(Speak as sneaking up with imaginary knife to kill #1. Actor #1 sees and avoids the knife.)*

1: "Pray and work."
3: In eighteen months, he mastered the Tamil language.
   In three years, he completed a translation of the New
   Testament, then a grammar and a dictionary, then a book
   for future missionaries on the culture and religions of
   southern India.
2: The first converts: five slaves.
1: The gospel preached to the poor!
3: The first Protestant church in India. 350 converts, a
   seminary, school, and printing press.
1: "Pray and work."
2: And death at age thirty-five. A very full life indeed.
1: Missions!
3: Let's do it too.

RECOMMENDED READING:

Scherer, James. "Bartholomew Ziegenbalg." *Missiology.*
   Oct. 1999.

THE MORAVIAN MISSIONARY MOVEMENT

(all heads bowed, then up with first line)

1: Missions!

2: The Moravian Revival of 1727.

3: Evangelical refugees, under Nicholas Zinzendorf, bound themselves together for world missions.

1: Praying in shifts for twenty-four hours a day, seven days a week, for more than 100 years!

2: Tent-making missions. Two grave diggers to Greenland. A potter and a carpenter to the West Indies.

3: Will someone go to Labrador for missions? *(turns to other actors and asks)*

1: Yes, I will go, if someone will please let me have a sturdy pair of shoes. *(Others nod in agreement)*

2: One in twelve Moravians became a missionary. *(points to or puts arm around #1)*

3: To the Virgin Islands, 1732.

2: Greenland, 1733.

3: Surinam, 1735.

2: South Africa, 1737.

1: North American Indians, 1740.

2: Jamaica and Antigua, 1750s.

3: Some joined with black slaves to evangelize them. *(#1 does some hoeing in ground, then looks up and says line)*

1: Three converts on the field for every church member at home.

2: Friedrich Martin and others imprisoned for ministering to black slaves on St. Thomas Island. Zinzendorf travels with some other Moravians, to plead their cause. He asks, *(walks with #1 as speaks toward #3, who has knelt with arms together, as if chained in prison)*

1: "What if the missionaries are already dead?"

2: "Well then, we can take their place."

3: The Moravians. Willing to go with whatever they had.

1: Missions. Let's do it too.

RECOMMENDED READING:

Greenfield, John. *When the Spirit Came: The Story of the Moravian Revival of 1727.* Bethany House, 1967.

Roth, Larry. "Count Nicholas Ludwig von Zinzendorf's Theory for Missions Portrayed at Herrnhut and by Selected 18th–20th Century Moravian Missions." S.T.M. Thesis, 1986; Theological Research Exchange Network, 1993.

Christian History Magazine (entire issue devoted to Moravians). Vol. 1, #1.

DAVID BRAINERD

(all heads bowed, then up with first line)

1: Missions!

2: David Brainerd. A student at Yale during the Great Awakening.

3: He dedicated himself to be a missionary to the Native Americans.

1: But they kicked him out of Yale for questioning the salvation of one of his tutors. Ah, David. You have much to learn. *(pushes #2 gently away; #2 clearly disturbed)*

2: But I will still pursue my calling. I want to evangelize the Indians.

3: Yes, work with this brother here. He will teach you how. *(takes #2 and points #2 to #1)*

2: No, I want to work alone with the Indians in New York. *(kindly, but firmly rejects offer)*

1: No fruit, discouragement. *(#2 clearly discouraged)*

3: Then to Indians in Pennsylvania. Same story . . . Brokenness. *(last word is key pivot point here; #2 with head in hands)*

1: Now God can use this man. *(put hand on #2 shoulder)*

2: To the Indians in New Jersey. *(lift head out of hands, encouraged with new vision)*

1: Intercession. Great outpouring of prayer. *(#2 kneels)*

3: Hours of prayer. In one instance, the snow melted around his kneeling body because of his sweat.

1: Revival! Converts. A great hunger for God's Word!

3: A diary written that still inspires today. *(#2 assumes writing positions, standing or sitting, and reads. This part on paper, not memorized, but read thoughtfully and passionately.)*

2: "All my concern is for the conversion of the heathen. I long and live to be a pilgrim, and want grace to imitate the life, labors, and sufferings of Paul among the heathen. I could think of undergoing the greatest sufferings, in the cause of Christ, with pleasure, that I might do something for their salvation, in distresses and deaths of any kind."

1: Tuberculosis and death at age twenty-nine. *(#2 bows head and closes eyes)*

3: David Brainerd. Passion, sacrifice.

2: Missions. Let's do it too. *(#2 raises his head for last line)*

RECOMMENDED READING:

Brainerd, David & Edwards, Jonathan (ed.). *The Life of Rev. David Brainerd*. Baker, 1983.

Day, Richard E. *Flagellant on Horseback: The Life Story of David Brainerd*. Judson, 1950.

Thornbury, John. *David Brainerd: Pioneer Mission to the American Indians*. Evangelical Press, 1996.

JOHN WILLIAMS
AND JOHN PATON

(all heads bowed, then up with first line)

1: Missions!

2: John Williams, John Paton: missionaries to the South Sea Islands.

3: Williams successfully evangelized cannibals.

1: He built a ship to evangelize neighboring tribes.

2: Beaten to death in 1839 and eaten by cannibals. *(#3 falls to ground as #2 speaks. #2 clenches fists and pretends pounding on #3 while speaking.)*

3: John Paton. *(gets up and gestures hand to #1)*

1: I must take his place.

2: His wife and son died within a year. *(#1 bows head in grief)*

3: Constant danger, disease, and loneliness.

2: And, opposition from witch doctors.

3: We are running out of water! *(#3 becomes chief and speaks this to other two actors)*

1: We must dig a well. We can get water that way. *(#1, as Paton, replies to #3)*

2: *(laugh)* One does not get water by digging. See how this man seeks to lead you away from my magic! *(witch doctor, shouts and points to #1)*

1: Then I will dig it myself. *(firm, but not rebellious)*

2: And we shall all see that your God is false. *(shouting to #1, then stand by #2 chief and silently murmur)*

1: "Oh Lord, let there be water." *(prays as he digs)*

3: And there was water! Fresh water. The chief and many others turned to the Lord. *(#3 bends down to see. "The chief" speaks as he pounds himself on chest, and then gestures behind him for "many others."*)

2: Later attempts by others to dig in the area only brought saltwater. *(no longer witch doctor)*

1: Paton translated the Bible into their language and trained about 300 native missionaries.

3: John Williams, John Paton.

2: Brave. Men of faith.

1: Missions. Let's do it too.

RECOMMENDED READING:

Paton, John G. *John G. Paton: Missionary to the New Hebrides.* Revell, 1898.

Upseth, Benjamin. *John Paton: Frontier Missionary to the South Pacific.* Bethany House, 1996.

For information on John Williams, see: Tucker, Ruth. *From Jerusalem to Irian Jaya: A Biographical History of Christian Missions.* Zondervan, 1983.

LOTTIE MOON

(all heads bowed, then up with first line)

1: Missions!

2: Lottie Moon: American missionary to China.

3: Single. She fought loneliness and discouragement.

1: Offer of marriage? *(spoken to #2 with outstretched hand)*

2: No, I will stay here at my post. *(kind refusal)*

3: Teaching children. *(gesture down with open arms to imaginary children)*

1: Traveling village to village, sharing the gospel. *(gesture outward to imaginary crowds)*

2: Thirty-five churches raised up through her work, training men to lead.

3: A copy of the Scriptures to Lee Sho Tin, famous Confucian scholar. He was saved and became an evangelist with more than 10,000 converts. *(hand #1 imaginary book, as #1 bows politely and receives)*

1: Missionary articles published in the United States.

3: Mother, Father! I have just read one of Miss Moon's articles. May I be a missionary, too? *(other two readers become listening parents who smile and respond to statement)*

2: A famine in her area. Food unable to be brought in. *(serious, sad)*

3: Lottie Moon stays, gives from her own small food supply to those in need.

1: Why doesn't she go home to America, where there is plenty of food? *(#1 as townsperson, spoken to #3)*

3: Miss Moon loves us. What we suffer, she suffers.

1: Then I know now that her gospel must be true. I will go and listen to the words of Jesus.

2: She dies of starvation on Christmas Eve, 1912.

3: Yes, we are her relatives. We have come to retrieve her belongings. *(stand with #1 and face #2)*

2: In this small sack is everything she owned. *(spoken with smile, without apology)*

3: There is nothing else? *(both #3 and #1 are very surprised)*

2: . . . no. *(again, spoken with smile)*

1: Lottie Moon. *(all three now position close facing audience)*

3: Total commitment.

2: Missions. Let's do it too.

RECOMMENDED READING:

International Mission Board, Southern Baptist Convention. *Journey Home: Lottie Moon of China.* (Videocassette, 26 min.). International Mission Board, 1997.

Rankin, Jerry. "Lottie Moon: A Legacy That Endures." *Commission.* Nov. 1995, pp. 4–15.

WILLIAM CAREY

(all heads bowed, then up with first line)

1: Missions!

2: William Carey, a shoemaker in England.

3: A poor businessman.

1: A mediocre preacher, an uninspiring teacher. Can God use this man?

2: He wrote a tract pleading for missionary efforts around the world.

3: How presumptuous! *(spoken with scorn)*

1: He founded a Baptist Missionary Society, with great effort and pleading.

2: "Young man, sit down, when God wants to convert the heathen, He will do it without your aid or mine!" *(shouts and points to #1)*

1: "Oh, but if you had only read about the Moravians, how they overcame all obstacles for Christ's sake, you would also go forward in faith." *(spoken to #2)*

3: Forty years in India without a furlough.

2: His wife gone mad. Children dying.

1: Poverty. Thieves, poisonous snakes, wild animals.

3: Seven years before his first convert.

2: On his deathbed. *(#1 takes seat and leans back, as if weak and dying. #2 and #3 become visitors at his deathbed who are bragging about Carey in his hearing.)*

3: What an amazing man! He has translated the Bible into six Indian dialects.

2: Portions of the Bible in twenty-nine others.

3: He also founded twenty-six churches, 126 schools.

2: And helped stop the dreadful custom of burning widows with their husbands.

1: "What is all this talk about William Carey? Carey this, Carey that. Won't anyone talk of William Carey's Savior? Come here my friends. On my tombstone, write my name, and these words, nothing else: 'A wretched, poor, and helpless worm. On Thy kind arms I fall.' " *(lines spoken in raspy, weak voice)*

2: William Carey. Humility, patience, fruit. *(pause before line, both #2 and #3 a little ashamed for their bragging, then thoughtfully speak this line)*

3: Missions. Let's do it too.

RECOMMENDED READING:

Carey, S. Pearce. *William Carey: The Father of Modern Missions*. London: Wakeman Trust, 1993.

George, Timothy. *Faithful Witness: The Life and Mission of William Carey*. New Hope, 1991.

Miller, Basil. *William Carey: Cobbler to Missionary*. Zondervan, 1952.

DRAMATIC
READINGS

ATTEMPT GREAT THINGS

by Shawn D. Haynie, © 1992

This reading is most effective as duet choral reading. The parts are indicated as such. However, it can be adapted for larger groups.

Some stage movement, which properly interprets the piece, is recommended, and some interpretation of the reading is given in italics.

MAN: Attempt great things for God!

WOMAN: Expect great things from God!

MAN: "Go ye into

TOGETHER: ALL THE WORLD

WOMAN: And preach the gospel

TOGETHER: TO EVERY CREATURE

MAN: Baptizing them in the name of the Father, Son, and Holy Spirit.

WOMAN: Teaching them to observe

TOGETHER: ALL THINGS

WOMAN: Whatsoever I have commanded you, and lo, I am with you ALWAY

TOGETHER: EVEN TO THE END OF THE AGE."

MAN: Attempt great things for God!

WOMAN: Expect great things from God!

MAN: "But ye shall receive

TOGETHER: POWER.

MAN: After that the Holy Spirit is come upon you

WOMAN: And ye shall be witnesses unto me

TOGETHER: IN JERUSALEM AND IN ALL JUDAEA.

MAN: "And suddenly there came a sound from heaven as a mighty rushing wind.

TOGETHER: THEY WERE FILLED WITH THE HOLY SPIRIT!

WOMAN: And there were dwelling at Jerusalem devout men who were amazed and marveled. Then Peter said,

MAN: 'Repent and be baptized every one of you in the name of Jesus Christ for the remission of sins.'

WOMAN: And the same day were added unto them

TOGETHER: ABOUT THREE THOUSAND SOULS.

MAN: And the Lord added to the church daily such as should be saved."

TOGETHER: *(starting in a whisper and growing in intensity)* JERUSALEM, JUDAEA, AND IN ALL SAMARIA

WOMAN: "Then Phillip went down to the city of Samaria and preached Christ unto them, and the people

TOGETHER: WITH ONE ACCORD

WOMAN: Gave heed to the things which Phillip spake."

TOGETHER: *(again starting as a whisper and growing)* JERUSALEM, JUDAEA, SAMARIA, AND UNTO THE UTTERMOST PART OF THE EARTH!

WOMAN: "Now there were at the church prophets and teachers. And as they ministered and fasted, the Holy Spirit said,

MAN: 'Separate unto Me Barnabas and Saul for the work whereunto I have called them.'"

WOMAN: Seleucia.

MAN: Paphos, where they withstood the sorcerer.

WOMAN: Perga.

MAN: Antioch of Pisidia.

WOMAN: Iconium.

MAN: Lystra, where Paul was stoned.

WOMAN: Derbe, home of Timothy, Paul's son in the faith.

TOGETHER: "IN ALL THESE CITIES—

TOGETHER: Confirming souls.

TOGETHER: Exhorting believers.

TOGETHER: Establishing churches.

TOGETHER: Ordaining elders."

WOMAN: Through this first missionary journey, the gospel
spread.

MAN: Throughout Africa by the Ethiopian Eunuch.

WOMAN: To Babylon, Persia, and India by Peter and Thomas.

MAN: To Rome.

WOMAN: To England.

MAN: The whole Western world.

TOGETHER: THE UTTERMOST PART OF THE EARTH.

MAN: In AD 375, the Emperor Constantine declared
Christianity the official religion of the Roman Empire!

(Long pause. Change to somber mood.)

MAN: The gospel is no longer spread by the word

WOMAN: But by the sword.

MAN: The evangelistic fire is nearly drowned out as ritual
replaces righteousness.

(Intensity once again begins to build.)

WOMAN: AD 1430

MAN: John Hus rekindles the flame, 1517.

WOMAN: Martin Luther spearheads the Protestant Reformation
and the gospel fire spreads, 1620.

MAN: The Puritans and Pilgrims bring the gospel to the New
World, 1730.

TOGETHER: The Great Awakening!

WOMAN: David Brainerd becomes the first American
missionary to the Indians.

MAN: David George goes to Nova Scotia.

WOMAN: George Liele pioneers a work to Jamaica.

TOGETHER: 1775!

(Again a long pause and return to somber mood.)

MAN: The Revolutionary War turns the thoughts of America and England away from missions and onto national survival.

WOMAN: The fire wanes.

(Again building in intensity.)

MAN: But even during this time God was working in the heart of a shoemaker in Paulersbury, England.

WOMAN: The Father of Modern Missions

TOGETHER: WILLIAM CAREY!

WOMAN: In his final address to the Baptist Mission Society of England, he said,

MAN: "Attempt Great Things for God!

WOMAN: Expect Great Things from God!"

(This next section is done in very rapid succession with great excitement.)

MAN: After his address, he headed for Bengal, India.

WOMAN: He mastered three Indian languages in seven years.

MAN: Translated the Bible into Bengali.

WOMAN: Established churches and medical missions.

MAN: In 1800, Carey moved to Serampore, India, and in his 34 years there he

WOMAN: Established a training center for incoming missionaries.

MAN: Established a print shop to publish Bibles and tracts.

WOMAN: Translated the entire Bible into four more Indian languages.

MAN: The New Testament into three additional languages.

WOMAN: Wrote a Bengali hymnbook.

MAN: Founded a Bible college to train Indian pastors.

WOMAN: Built a hospital that cared for body and soul.

MAN: And, every day, preached to the people!

WOMAN: William Carey had fanned the flames and missions was growing with every passing decade.

MAN: Among those influenced by Carey—Adoniram Judson—Father of American Missions.

WOMAN: Hudson Taylor—founder of the China Inland Mission.

MAN: The legendary David Livingstone.

WOMAN: Pioneer missionary women—Amy Carmichael and Mary Slessor.

MAN: John and Betty Stamm—missionary martyrs—as well as Jim Elliot and Nate Saint.

WOMAN: Don Richardson—author of *Peace Child*.

MAN: Otto Koning—who can forget *The Pineapple Story*?

WOMAN: *Daktar*—Viggo Olsen.

TOGETHER: THOUSANDS UPON THOUSANDS WERE SAVED!

MAN: Attempt Great Things for God!

WOMAN: Expect Great Things from God!

TOGETHER: BUT TODAY!

(A long pause and again a somber mood.)

MAN: Churches build multi-million dollar edifices and drop the missions budget because "they can't afford it."

WOMAN: Missionaries leave their fields of service for lack of support.

MAN: Within the next 10 years, over 50% of the missionaries currently serving will reach retirement age.

WOMAN: Only one person enters career missions for every five who leave.

MAN: Christian colleges cancel missions-related courses for "lack of interest."

WOMAN: Enlistment personnel find it harder to recruit new missionaries.

MAN: The flame is dying.

WOMAN: Over 10,000 language groups are still without a spoken or written witness.

MAN: Flickering

WOMAN: Urban areas around the world are growing faster than already established churches can handle.

MAN: Growing dim

(Now begin growing in intensity.)

TOGETHER: HOW CAN WE REKINDLE THE FIRE?

WOMAN: "But seek ye first the kingdom of God and His righteousness"

MAN: Don't ask "Should I go?" but, rather, "In light of God's commands, should I stay?"

WOMAN: Not "Should I give?" but "How much and to whom should I give?"

MAN: As the evangelist of old did, draw a circle on the ground, step inside, and then ask God to send a revival to everyone in the circle.

WOMAN: Pray with the missionary who said, "Lord Jesus, take me, send me, use me."

MAN: Attempt great things for God!

WOMAN: Expect great things from God!

TOGETHER: WILL YOU HELP KEEP THE FIRE OF MISSIONS ALIVE?

It is my desire to have this piece used for live performance to challenge people with the past and future of missions.

I grant permission to any individual, church, or mission organization to copy and perform this reading for live performance provided the performers do not do it for hire nor is it recorded for sale.

For further information, please contact me by e-mail: sdhaynie@terra.cl

Shawn D. Haynie
Baptist Mid-Missions
Serving in Santiago, Chile

CONVERSATIONS WITH THE FATHER

by Becky Staab

A reading for two people:

The lines beginning with "Father" are to be read by a woman representing a missionary. The word "Father" is said at the beginning as part of her prayer.

The lines beginning with "Child" are to be read by a man representing the voice of God. The word "Child" is said at the beginning as part of God's response to His child.

The Scripture references are intended as background material and are not meant to be read aloud.

Father, my cook just broke my last glass bowl and I can't replace
    it here!
Child, stop looking at things which can be seen. They are just
    temporal; look at the unseen. That is what is eternal.
Father, help me to "hold lightly things of this earth,
    Transient treasures, what are they worth?
    Moths can corrupt them, rust can decay,
    All their bright beauty fades in a day.
    Let me hold lightly things that are mine,
    Lord, Thou didst give me all that is Thine."
    (excerpt from Martha Snell Nicholson's poem)

Father, my husband is overwhelmed and I don't know how to
    encourage him.

Child, remember I make all things work together for good to
    those who love Me and are called according to My purpose.
    And don't forget that purpose: to make you like My Son.
    My Spirit Himself will intercede for you when you don't
    know how to pray. *(Romans 8:26–29)*

Father, teach me to see and affirm all my husband is and has
    "in Christ"; help both of us to rest in that "hope of glory."
    (Colossians 1:27)

Father, all around me I see so many good and needful things I
    could do. I don't know how to discern Your voice and will.

Child, have you forgotten My promise to give My wisdom
    generously and without reproach to anyone who asks?
    (James 1:5)

Father, forgive me for forgetting. I ask You now to help me to
    be still and know that You are God; to see clearly where You
    are at work and humbly ask how I can have a part in what
    You are doing; to listen carefully and hear clearly Your still
    small voice. Help me to see Your plan to make Yourself
    known to all peoples of the world. *(Psalm 46:10)*

Father, I don't have strength to keep going. I'm weary in doing
    well.

Child, remember it is the joy of the Lord that is your strength.

Father, teach me to rejoice in Your perfection and so find
    strength.

Father, I don't have confidence I can do all the tasks before me.

Child, you are wise not to be confident in yourself, but you can
    have complete confidence in Christ *(2 Corinthians 3:4, 5).*

Father, teach me to have confidence in the complete adequacy
    of Your work through me.

Father, there's another person at my door, someone poor or
   with an unsolvable problem, no doubt. Why is there so
   much trouble in the world? I don't have any answers for
   all these needs!
Child, both your hope and theirs can only be found in Me.
Father, teach me to focus my hope on You as David did.
   Why do I weep? Why do I mourn?
   Why does it seem that God is not found?
   Why am I in despair and confusion of soul?
   Why does it seem that evil abounds?
   God of my hope, O God of my life,
   God of my strength, O God of my joy
   In You will I hope: You are my help; You are my God.
   (adapted from Psalm 42:5, 11)

Father, I am such a failure. I just don't measure up to any kind
   of a missionary at all!
Child, My people who are called by My name must humble
   themselves. *(2 Chronicles 7:14)* Mine is the kingdom, the
   power, and the glory. *(Matthew 6:13)*
Father, teach me to recognize the pride that seeks significance,
   success, and honor for myself. Help me to confess it and
   repent of it. Teach me, like Christ, to only seek Your glory.
   (John 7:18)

Father, my heart is shriveled up, dry, and loveless. I can't love
   these people!
Child, "apart from Me you can do nothing. Abide in MY love."
   (John 15:5, 9)
Father,
   "I love, my God, but with no love of mine,
   For I have none to give:
   I love Thee, Lord, but all the love is Thine,
   For by Thy life I live.

I am as nothing, and rejoice to be
Emptied and lost and swallowed up in Thee."
(excerpt from Madame Jeanne Marie Guyon)

Father, these people are so manipulative and quick to take
  advantage. I'm tired of feeling so stupid, unable to
  communicate well or understand the subtleties of this
  culture! I'm tired of being dependent on them to do things
  I did for myself (the way I wanted to) at home. I don't want
  to be so vulnerable!
Child, for you I became a helpless, dependent baby. I laid aside
  the rights of My deity, which included power and control.
  I didn't even instantly become an influential leader. I started
  with the complete dependence of a newborn. And I was
  certainly misunderstood.
Father, teach me to willingly accept vulnerability out of love
  for You, and to rejoice in fellowship with You through
  this thing that is difficult for me. If You accepted such
  vulnerability for me, surely I can do this little thing for You!

Father, I just don't ever achieve the Christ-likeness I think I
  should.
Child, you can't achieve it by yourself. You must learn to let
  Christ fill and consume you, like that burning bush which
  Moses saw, until all that people see when they look at you
  is Me.
Father, I pray today with St. Patrick
    "Christ with me, Christ before me,
    Christ behind me, Christ in me,
    Christ beneath me, Christ above me,
    Christ on my right, Christ on my left,
    Christ when I lie down, Christ when I sit down, Christ
      when I arise,
    Christ in the heart of every man who thinks of me,

Christ in the mouth of everyone who speaks of me,
Christ in every eye that sees me,
Christ in every ear that hears me."

Father, I feel so lonely. I don't have any real friends. No one really cares about me.

Child, before you knew Me I loved you. Every day I wait to spend time with you.

Father, as Moses prayed, "Pardon me and take me for Your inheritance" *(Exodus 34:9).* Teach me to live in a constant awareness of Your presence, talking and listening to You all day long, rejoicing in Your love and returning my love and worship to You.

Father, I am discouraged. I never seem to make any progress in my work and I've lost the motivation to keep going.

Child, I have not destined you for wrath but to obtain salvation and life through Christ. His return is your source of encouragement *(I Thessalonians 5: 9–11).* These daily set-backs, lack of progress, and frustrations are part of living in hope of the future fulfillment and perfection I have prepared for you. Not yet! Wait in hope with perseverance. *(Romans 8:18–25)*

Father, teach me to focus beyond the immediate frustrations to the final fulfillment You have already accomplished and will one day reveal. Thank You for the first fruits of the Spirit through which we gain occasional glimpses of the glory that will be revealed. But Father, teach me also while I wait, to work and pray for those for whom Your return now would be a final judgment—not a fulfillment of hope.

Becky and her husband, David, serve at
Memorial Christian Hospital in Bangladesh.

ALL'S WELL AT THE WELL

by Julie Sanders

Written when Julie and her husband, Jeff, were ABWE appointees to the Philippines

I've just returned from the well. You might think my burden is heavy, that my load would bear down on me, but it does not. Not that it never has done so. In days gone by, I would return from the well with a heart that weighed on me like the tent of a shepherd or a cedar of Lebanon. You see, though my shoulders were sore with the weight of my load, it was never enough for the unquenchable thirst of the men who received it. The water seemed to me to only rearrange the smears of the dirt on the hands of the children who played in the dust around the feet of their mothers. My tasks seemed to lack meaning or purpose. They seemed to be so temporary. At times, I would rally myself to be determined to carry more and to do it with determination that would honor even the great judge Deborah. Still, it was the deeper burdens of life that hung heavily on my heart as I listened to the cares of the other women.

- The widow who mourns without end the loss of her husband and longs for her youth.
- The young mother who briefly escaped her babies, complaining over the endless needs of her brood, while decrying the ever-present advances of her energetic husband. She was so desperate she considered adding another wife to bear the load.

- The woman who brings her father's waterpot, longing for a husband of her own.
- And the somber sister, whose son is far from home and is—some say—a prodigal who has yet to return.

Our hearts would stir one another with our miseries and pains, and we would find ourselves heavy-hearted at the well, leaving with no true refreshment. We found no reason to sing praise. Perhaps you have been to such a well and carried such a burden. Let me tell you, today, I have much cause for praise.

The well, you see, is still the same distance. The rope, still as long and as unyielding. The sun, just as hot at the sixth hour as ever. And I still carry water to the same thirsty men and the same dirty children. But the burdens to and from and around the well will never be the same. Something happened that has changed the journey and the destination. In fact, the women of Galilee with whom I draw water from day to day agree that they, too, will never be the same. You see, we met a great Man who became our Teacher. But more than that, I discovered that this great Rabbi, Jesus, is the true Messiah I have waited for. Have you also looked for Him? The great truth is: He is ALIVE for ME.

Maybe women of your day have not heard or don't believe events from long ago. But I was there, and I know it to be true. He is alive for me. This proves God's love for me is deep enough that He gave all He had: the Lord Jesus Christ. Let me tell you about HIM.

- He came to serve and to show He is God's Son.
- He lived a perfect life, died, and was buried.
- He conquered death.
- He arose and lives for me.
- He wants me to know He'll return for me.

Yes, God's love for me is deep. God's plan for me is real. Life is full of hope when He is in control. Now let me tell you how I know this is true. We women followed Jesus and knew such joy in being with Him. Journeys to the well became ways in which to serve when the Master was at the other end. All of us women agreed He had a way of calming our fears and giving meaning to our tasks and our trials. With Him, we had hope.

We had just celebrated the Passover before the Teacher, Jesus, was arrested in the Garden. The disciples who were His closest followers had been with Him, but they have told us of the night when they "all forsook Him and fled." Since the moment when the disciples left the mob in the garden, we had all lived in fear and sorrow. The events that followed pierce my heart as I recall the news of Judas' hanging, the release of Barabbas, the untreated bruises and cuts on the Master's body. Finally, the mocking of the chief priests, scribes, and elders. Then the terrifying shaking of the earth, the release of the dead from their graves, and the great darkness. I, along with the other women who followed Jesus, watched from afar. We were filled with such fear and deep desperation. While He had been with us, we felt great safety and comfort. His presence was sat-isfying, gave us purpose, and filled us with hope. With His death came the fear that the burdens of our lives were all ours once again. Had Caesar's power conquered in the end? Our lives seemed without reason once more, and the well became, once again, a meeting place for pain. Seeing only the darkness and our grief, we could find no cause for praise. How would you have felt?

For three days, the Lord Jesus lay in the tomb of Joseph of Arimathea, a council member. The promised One, the hope of all Israel was crucified and crushed. During those days, we mourned His death and the return and triumph of our trouble. Perhaps you know such mourning. I was so eager to do some-thing, to express my love for Him, to find comfort, and to be of service to the One who had served us with such humility. My distress made it hard to sleep, and so I awoke very early. Along with several others, I went to bring spices to anoint our Lord

After the Sabbath, as the first day of the week began to
dawn, we women came to see the tomb. There was a great
earthquake; for an angel of the Lord descended from heaven,
and came and rolled back the stone from the door, and sat on
it. His countenance was like lightning, and his clothing as white
as snow. And the guards shook for fear of him, and became like
dead men. But the angel answered and said to us, "Do not be
afraid, for I know that you seek Jesus who was crucified. He is
not here; for He is risen, as He said."

Then the angel showed us where the Lord had laid and
then told us to go quickly and tell the disciples, the eleven who
remained. We left, running with fear and great joy. Then, on our
way, we saw Jesus, the Son of God. "Rejoice!" He said, and we
fell at His feet and worshipped Him. Even when the disciples
were reluctant to believe, even when I began to doubt, our
human frailty did not change the fact that the One whom we
saw despised, beaten, and crucified overcame death and is truly
alive.

Never will my life be the same. Never will I go to the well
or hear of life's cares or bear a burden again in the same way I
did before. The angel knew we were full of fear. He spoke to
our confusion, to the uncertainty and insecurity we faced as
frail women of flesh and blood. I believe women of all ages
know this feeling.

Not only were we afraid of the angel and the quaking of
the earth, but we were filled with fear that a dead Jesus can not
save us. A dead man can not hear our cries. A dead man has
no power over those who oppress us, betray us, or misuse us.
A dead man can not give us hope. In the long days after the
hours at Golgotha, our lack of faith was proven as we were
filled with fears for that day and for our future. We felt such
defeat, such helplessness, and such unquenchable sadness. But
the morning at the tomb changed all that. "Do not be afraid,"
the angel said. "He is not here. For He is risen, as He said."

Yes, He had said that. And, truly, God's love for me is deep enough to give all. He gave His life for me. I saw Him hang there between the thieves as the Jewish leaders gloated and laughed. I saw the soldiers tear his robes and spit on him. God's *love* for me is deep enough to give His all.

God's *plan* for me is real. If the Lord Jesus had not risen, what difference would just another dead man make in my life, in my future, in my eternity? And what difference would another dead man make in the lives of women in times to come as they journey to and from their wells and pour out the burdens of their lives to one another? And what reason would we have to praise? But "He is not here," the angel said, "He is risen." We are not helpless. We are not beaten. We are not alone. With His resurrection, His life proved that He was who He claimed to be, and that He has power over death, over pain, over the Caesars of my day and of every age to come.

"For as in Adam all die, even so in Christ all shall be made alive. . . . For He must reign till He has put all enemies under His feet. The last enemy that will be destroyed is death."

Life is now full of *hope* because I know God is in control. "Behold, I tell you a mystery: We shall not all sleep, but we shall all be changed, in a moment, in the twinkling of an eye, at the last trump: for the trumpet will sound, and the dead will be raised incorruptible, and we shall all be changed. . . . But thanks be to God, who gives us the victory through our Lord Jesus Christ. Therefore, . . . be steadfast, unmovable, always abounding in the work of the Lord, knowing that your labor is not in vain in the Lord." Our future is, indeed, secure, full of promise, because God is in control.

When Jesus died on the cross, I was so afraid the rulers of the earth really did have all authority. But before the Lord Jesus ascended to heaven to be with His Father, some of us gathered on the mountain. There Jesus said, "All power is given to Me in heaven and in earth. Go ye therefore, and teach all nations, bap-

tizing them in the name of the Father, and of the Son, and of
the Holy Spirit: teaching them to observe all things whatsoever
I have commanded you; and lo, I am with you always, even to
the end of the age."

"Blessed be the God and Father of our Lord Jesus Christ,
who according to His abundant mercy has begotten us again to
a living hope through the resurrection of Jesus Christ from the
dead, to an inheritance incorruptible, and undefiled, and that
does not fade away, reserved in heaven for you, who are kept
by the power of God through faith unto salvation ready to be
revealed in the last time. In this you greatly rejoice, though now
for a season, if need be, you are in heaviness through manifold
temptations, that the trial of your faith, being much more pre-
cious than gold that perishes, though it be tried by fire, might
be found unto praise, and honor, and glory at the appearing of
Jesus Christ, whom having not seen, you love. Though now you
see Him not, yet believing, you rejoice with joy inexpressible
and full of glory, receiving the end of your faith, even the
salvation of your souls."

I can serve Him now each day and trust my future to Him
because He is the One who has all authority. He proved it
when He arose from Joseph's tomb and left the grave clothes
behind to walk among us. He will always be with me. And He
will always be with you, as you journey to your well, and as
you lift the rope of your life with your sisters who gather there
with you. *God's love for me is deep enough to give all for me. His
plan for me is real. And life is full of hope when He is in control.*

Some day, all of us who saw this with our own eyes will be
asleep. But the apostle John explained to us why he wrote the
gospel that bears his name: "These things have been written
that you may believe that Jesus is the Christ, the Son of God,
and that believing you may have life in His name."

Throughout ages to come, women will still bear burdens,
water their sheep and their camels and their husbands who

thirst as camels. And though they have not seen the Lord Jesus, they too can have hope. I pray they'll understand the things I have said and rejoice, as the Master told me to when I worshiped at His feet. I pray they will live with the hope of redemption and Christ's soon return. This surely will give them cause for praise!

RECOMMENDED READING:

The Bible verses used throughout this reading are listed in the order they appear:

Matthew 27:55
Mark 15:43
Matthew 26:56
Matthew 27:41
Matthew 27:51, 52
Mark 16: 1
Matthew 28:1-10
John 20:1-18
I Corinthians 15:22, 25, 26
I Corinthians 15:51, 52, 57, 58
Matthew 28:18-20
1 Peter 1:3-9
John 20:30

RESPONSE TO THE LORD:

What cares have you brought to the well? I have battled with uncertainty and even fear during the past two years as the Lord has taken us on a journey of going farther for Him. The things I've shared with you have been the things I have been learning, things God has been showing me and making real to me.

I wonder what my life will be like, how my family will adjust to living in a foreign land, what our future will be. I have asked myself,

"Is the truth that my God conquered death for me and now lives enough?

Enough to uproot our lives?

Enough to give us comfort in the darkest times?

Enough to give us meaning each day when we are the strangers?

Will it be enough to make us press on?

Am I leaving all I love, or am I following the One I love?"

Think over these questions as they apply to your life. Listen to God, and respond to His leading as He uses His truth to give you a cause for praise that will not fade.

DRAMAS

AMAZON LIFE AT THE
PORT OF TWO BROTHERS

by Betty Neumayer with Paul Schlener

Music: Open with jungle music playing, then as lights darken, play Christian music until the narrator begins.

NARRATOR: We start our adventure in the lives of two brothers called to spread the Good News along the Amazon River. John and Paul Schlener had just applied to the Association of Baptists for World Evangelism to become missionaries to the Ticuna Indians in Brazil. The year was 1950. Dr. Harold Commons is talking with associate Robert Burns.

SCENE ONE

Two men sitting around a desk with a map of the world in a prominent place.

DR. COMMONS: Those Schlener brothers are intent on going into the wildest part of the Amazon jungle. I don't know if we can approve their going to such a remote area.

MR. BURNS: No one has ever gone into that area before, and no one knows the language of the people.

DR. COMMONS: Yes, and John and Paul have wives, and each has two small children. There is no plane in the area for emergencies. It will be hard even to keep in touch with them. Riverboats carry everything that goes into the jungle—even the mail.

MR. BURNS: Leticia, Colombia, is the nearest town, and it is 100 miles up river. There's one good piece of news,

however; our missionary, Orville Floden, has located a piece
of property near a little village called Santa Rita. It's 525 feet
on the riverfront and a mile deep into the jungle.

DR. COMMONS: Yes, I hear that property is in the center of a
1,000 mile area that has no Christian witness to the Indians
along the river.

MR. BURNS: That's an ideal situation for evangelism but a
dangerous place to live.

DR. COMMONS: There are poisonous snakes and mosquitoes
carrying malaria. It won't be a picnic to settle there.

MR. BURNS: They'll have to build their own houses, too.

DR. COMMONS: The Schleners have just graduated from the
Bible Institute of Los Angeles and they are raring to go.
If the Lord is in this, we must give permission.

MR. BURNS: I think we should send them out on deputation
and see how the Lord leads. One indication of God's calling
will be the results of their ministry before they ever get to
the Amazon. Let's see if they can challenge churches to pray
for them and meet their financial needs.

SCENE TWO

PAUL *and* JESSIE *at the airport.*

Music: Airport sounds, then fading as narrator begins.

NARRATOR: One year later—1951. Deputation is over and
the two families are packed and ready to leave for South
America. We find Paul and Jessie struggling with the last
load of luggage at the airport.

JESSIE: Paul, did you bring a shower curtain among all those
things we packed?

PAUL: Oh, Jessie, how would I know? I had so many things
to pack and so many details to take care of.

JESSIE: I suppose you expect me to bathe in the Amazon River with crocodiles and piranhas and snakes and all those squirmy things?

PAUL: It will be so hot down there you'll be glad to jump right into the river along with all those squirmy things.

JESSIE: I'll bet John remembered a shower curtain for Fran. You should have thought of it, Paul.

PAUL: It's okay, Honey. I did think of it. *(out loud to himself)* At least I did *think* of it.

SCENE THREE

JOHN *and* PAUL *in a boat.*

Music: Jungle music begins, then fades for narrator.

NARRATOR: The longest river in the world becomes the Schleners' only road. They must go up or down it everywhere they go since the jungle is too thick to travel in very far. These boat rides for supplies and ministry trips give John and Paul time for conversation and contemplation.

JOHN: Well, Paul, our houses are finally finished. Now we must start thinking about building a church and a school.

PAUL: Yes, John. Our wives and kids have pretty well adjusted and settled in. People here really need a school. Because the natives can't read or count, the riverboat captains take advantage of them when they try to sell rubber and dried fish. They really get cheated.

JOHN: I think we must get some kind of education started here. Since nobody knows how to read, we will probably have both the kids and their parents in school. Then we must get the Bible translated into their language.

PAUL: Wow! That will be quite a job, John. We have to learn the language ourselves first.

JOHN: The Lord has really given us a big job here. If we stopped to think about it we would probably catch the first boat home, wouldn't we?

PAUL: You're right. But the Lord has been so faithful in getting us here and providing us a good relationship with the local people. They really need a school in addition to some good preaching.

JOHN: Fran and Jessie could teach school and also give the kids music and singing lessons.

PAUL: Jessie used to be a drum majorette in school. She brought her baton and could start a marching band. And we could cut a clearing out of the jungle to make a soccer field since it is such a popular sport down here.

JOHN: The school could lead into teaching people about the Lord and what He has done for them. You know that young boy who shows such amazing musical talent, Evandro Batista? He seems to be able to play most any instrument he picks up. Fran has been helping him with her accordion. It is certainly a miracle to find a little boy in the jungle who can play musical instruments so well.

PAUL: Evandro has a good singing voice, too. We must encourage him. He would make a wonderful witness of God's grace to the world.

JOHN: *(Steering the boat in a sudden sharp motion)* Oh, Oh! There's one of those big crocs. They look just like a big northern Idaho tamarack log floating in the water. We'd better be careful.

NARRATOR: John and Paul can tell many stories of conversions to Christ and lives changed by the Gospel. Let's meet Raimundo, an unfortunate young Ticuna boy.

(Off stage RAIMUNDO—pronounced Himundo—comes down the aisle yelling.)

RAIMUNDO: Senhor Paulo, Senhor Paulo. *(He advances down the aisle and waits for* PAUL *to speak before he repeats his call.)*

SCENE FOUR

In front of PAUL'*s house.*

PAUL: *(Out loud to himself)* Here comes that skinny, sickly kid Raimundo, from out in the jungle. He's sick from smoking too much and drinking rum, and I think he also has malaria. *(as* RAIMUNDO *approaches the stage,* PAUL *calls out)*

PAUL: *Bom dia,* Raimundo. What can I do for you this morning?

RAIMUNDO: Senhor Paulo, my father is very sick with fever. Can you come to see him?

PAUL: Raimundo, it is good you're so concerned about your father.

RAIMUNDO: It is a little walk in the jungle to reach my home. We have to go through the village to get there.

PAUL: You caught me at good time, Raimundo. I have just finished sharpening my machete. You sit here for a minute while I will gather my things, and I'll go with you.

*(*PAUL *gathers his knife, machete, Bible, and small medical kit and follows* RAIMUNDO *off the stage.)*

Jungle music comes on quite loud and fades when the narrator begins.

NARRATOR: Paul and the boy arrive at Raimundo's home in the jungle. Since his father, Manuel, is very ill, Raimundo's mother is about to go hunting for their food. We find her loading her gun with powder and smoking a pipe at the same time. When she sees Senhor Paulo arriving, she puts out her pipe and puts it in her gunpowder pouch. The expected explosion does not occur. Evidently she was used to doing it that way.

SCENE FIVE

Begins inside the hut: After pausing to watch MANUEL's *wife loading her gun,* PAUL *and* RAIMUNDO *walk inside to find* MANUEL *on a cot.*

PAUL: Sorry to hear you are sick, Manuel. Where do you hurt?

MANUEL: Ah, Senhor Paulo, I hurt all over, but my back is always hurting. A tree fell on me years ago, and I have never been able to straighten up since. But it is the fever that bothers me most right now.

PAUL: You know I am not a doctor, Manuel, but I will do what I can for you. (PAUL *gives the man a shot and kneels to talk to him*) I hear, Manuel, that you chant prayers for people who are brought to you.

MANUEL: Yes, that is true, Senhor Paulo. I specialize in babies.

PAUL: Then you must have some idea about God. I am always interested to know other people's ideas about God. What do you think about God, Manuel?

MANUEL: Oh, I have faith in God. We all have to have a God for this or that.

PAUL: Manuel, let me tell you what God did for you. He realized you were a sinner and had to pay for those sins. That's why He sent His only Son, the Lord Jesus Christ, to die in your place and cleanse you from your sins so that you can go to Heaven when you die. You know that God has done so much for my brother, John, and me and our families that we wanted to come here and tell you about Jesus, God's Son. You think about these things, Manuel, and feel free to call for me to come any time.

MANUEL: Thank you, Senhor Paulo. God will pay you for this visit.

PAUL: God bless you, Manuel. Goodbye for now.

Music on for scene change, but fades for narrator.

NARRATOR: Paul is returning from the jungle where he has
been cutting wood for a boat. It has been several weeks
since his visit to Raimundo's father. He arrives to find Jessie
sifting the worms out of the flour in preparation for making
the family's weekly bread supply. Her mood doesn't appear
to be the best!

SCENE SIX

In PAUL *and* JESSIE's *house.*

JESSIE: It would serve you right some day if I just didn't sift the
worms out of this flour and just baked the bread—worms
and all.

PAUL: What's the matter with you this morning, Jessie? You've
had worms in your flour ever since we got here. What's so
different about today?

JESSIE: Oh, it's so hot, and the mosquitoes are terrible, and I got
scared by a big snake right by the back door this morning,
and you haven't brought home any turtles lately. The last
one you got must have been a male 'cause it didn't have any
eggs in it.

PAUL: I guess John and I could go turtle hunting if that would
make you happy.

(Pause while JESSIE *sifts.)*

JESSIE: Paul, did you teach those boys in school to erase the
pencil marks on their papers with the heels of their tennis
shoes? It sounds like something you would do.

PAUL: No, I didn't exactly *teach* them that. I just told them
erasers were made out of the rubber they get from the trees

around here. They do look funny, don't they, when they put their feet up on the desk to erase something? It was a wonderful thing though, wasn't it, when the riverboats brought the first tennis shoes the kids had ever seen?

JESSIE: And how about the boys sharpening their pencils in school with their machetes? It seems dangerous to me. And when you are working on your light plant and you change oil, they ask for the crank case oil so they can use it for hair oil. They think they look so great. They sure do some funny things. Now go and study. I want to get this dough in the oven.

(PAUL *sits down with his Bible and reads a while. Along comes* RAIMUNDO.)

RAIMUNDO: Hello, Senhor Paulo. Are you very busy?

PAUL: *Bom dia,* Raimundo. How is your Dad today?

RAIMUNDO: My father is much worse, Senhor Paulo. He wants to see you again. Can you come?

PAUL: Sure thing, Raimundo. Let's go. (PAUL *gathers his things and leaves with* RAIMUNDO)

Music comes on, then fades when the narrator begins.

NARRATOR: Paul and Raimundo made another trip to Raimundo's home in the jungle. Manuel is much worse and is anxious to talk to Paul. Once again we see Paul Schlener as a missionary, a doctor, and a friend.

SCENE SEVEN

RAIMUNDO'*s home in the jungle.*

PAUL: *(as he approaches* MANUEL'*s cot)* How are you, Senhor Manuel?

MANUEL: Not so good, not so good. I am getting much
weaker.

PAUL: Would you like me to take you up the river to the
doctor, Manuel? He would be able to help you much better
than I can.

MANUEL: No doctor, no more medicine, Senhor Paulo. It's no
use. When you were here before you talked about being
saved by God. I want you to tell me more about that.

PAUL: *(moving closer to* MANUEL*)* My pleasure, Manuel. Hard
as it may seem for you to understand, God really does love
you. He loves you as much as He loves me and my family.
Then you ask, if God loves me, why does he let me suffer
like this? Manuel, if you were well and strong, you would
probably not let me come and explain the plan of salvation
to you. Let me show you what it says in the Bible. "For by
grace you are saved through faith, and that not of yourself,
it is the gift of God." Another Bible verse tells us that God
showed His love for us in this way: "While we were yet
sinners, Christ died for us." The verse in Acts 16:31 tells us
what to do. It says, "Believe on the Lord Jesus Christ and
you will be saved." And listen to this one, "The wages of
sin is death; but the gift of God is eternal life through Jesus
Christ our Lord." Christ died on the cross for all sinners.
He died for you, Manuel. If you believe that Christ died for
your sins and accept the gift of salvation, you, too, will go
to heaven when you leave this world. Let me read one more
verse, this time from John 1:12, "As many as received Him,
to them God gave the power to become the sons of God,
even to them that believe on his name."

MANUEL: Senhor Paulo, I want to accept this gift of salvation.
I always knew there was a God who was real. I just didn't
know how to approach Him.

*(*PAUL *kneels beside the cot and* MANUEL *prays to receive Christ.
Music is playing during this time.)*

MANUEL: Senhor Paulo, thanks for coming and telling me
about the Lord Jesus Christ. I have found peace about
dying, but I am worried about Raimundo. He cannot read
or write, and he is not well. Could you take him to your
school and teach him? We have no money to pay for this.

PAUL: I will find a job for him, and he can work for me and go
to school, too. Don't you worry about him, Manuel."

(PAUL says goodbye to MANUEL and walks away.)

SCENE EIGHT

JOHN *and* PAUL *in the boat.*

NARRATOR: Some years have passed now. The village has
changed under the constant care and ministry of the two
Schlener families. We join Paul and John on the river again.
This time they are fishing for supper and reflecting on the
Lord's goodness.

JOHN: Paul, do you think we have enough fish yet?

PAUL: I think maybe we do. How many can your family eat,
John? Maybe 10 or 12? I think we ought to go turtle
hunting, too. That gives us a little change of diet. The family
really gets excited when we bring home a turtle.

JOHN: The kids are really doing well in school, aren't they?
Ever since Raimundo's father died and the boy is earning
a little money, his health has improved. He's been saved and
is already talking of going away to Bible School. I think he
will make a fine preacher. And Evandro is talking of Bible
school, too. With his musical talent, he will be a good
witness for the Lord.

PAUL: And others are going off to school, too. I guess shaking
hands with up to 1,000 people every church service is
beginning to pay off. Our object was to come down here

and teach the way of God to the natives so that someday they could teach their own people. Along the way, we have made wonderful friends whom we'll see in heaven someday.

JOHN: Yes, the Lord has been good in allowing us to serve Him here. *(sound of bell off stage)* Oh, Oh, I hear the dinner bell ringing. Guess we better get off this river. Okay, Brother?

SCENE NINE

A small pulpit facing the audience.

NARRATOR: Many years have gone by since the last scene. Raimundo turned out to be a good student and has finished Bible school. He is married now and pastors a church. He has been invited to speak here at First Baptist Church—a church which sponsored the Schlener families at the Port of Two Brothers. This is the church's Annual Missionary Conference. Remember the first time Paul told us about Raimundo? And now I am pleased and happy to introduce to you Pastor Raimundo Freita Braga, all the way from South America. Welcome, Raimundo.

(RAIMUNDO approaches the pulpit and speaks humbly.)

RAIMUNDO: Friends, I am so happy to be here today. I was as far down at the bottom as I could get until God brought two brothers to the Amazon River. They didn't know us Ticunas when they came, but they loved us anyway. They were good to us and taught us what God did for us when He sent His only Son to die for our sins. We had been waiting to hear that all of our lives.

It was good that people in North America sent the Schlener families to give us the Word of God. Your prayers and your money sent them to our village and kept them there through all kinds of hardships so that the Lord's work could be accomplished in our lives. I now serve God in my own church in Manaus, Brazil, and my wife teaches in a Christian school. My friend Evandro Batista is an ABWE missionary in Portugal. Many other of our friends have gone on to Bible school and are in the Lord's work today.

If the Schlener brothers had not come, thousands of us along the Amazon River would never have been told of God's love for them. And just think, you had a part in sending them. Then you had blessings for yourselves by praying for them. God works in wonderful ways through missionaries all over the world. I challenge you to pray and to seek what the Lord has for you to do and where He would have you serve Him. I believe the time is short before the Lord Jesus comes again. Thank you for sending God's Word to us on the Amazon at the Port of Two Brothers. God bless you all.

THE STATUS QUO

A Humorous Missionary Skit with a Serious Message

*by Jack Shiflett, ABWE Executive Administrator for
Western Europe*

Props:

- A sign large enough to be clearly read all over the
  auditorium. Place it on the platform or on the wall.
  Write these words on the sign:

  WESTERN EUROPE

  Unhidden but Unreached

- A barrier. This can be a table or a wall approximately
  3 feet high and 6 feet wide. On the table covering or side
  of the barrier, write these words: Post Christian, Secular,
  Humanistic, Occultism, Skepticism, Materialism, Egoism,
  Hedonism, Apathy, Neo-pagan.
- Two suitcases or boxes, approximately 10 inches high by
  2 feet long, with words written large enough to be clearly
  read all over the auditorium. Write "STATUS" on one
  box and "QUO" on the other.
- Two chairs for the man and woman seated behind the
  barrier.
- Pith helmet for the missionary.
- A pulpit and glass of water.
- A hand full of "tracts" (cut up paper).

(Enter MISSIONARY *singing: "Give me that old time religion, give
me that old time religion . . . it was good for Paul and Silas and
it's good enough for me." The* MISSIONARY *is dressed in a pith*

59

helmet and carrying the two boxes with the words "STATUS" and "QUO." Singing, he approaches the barrier, turns to speak to the audience.)

MISSIONARY: Hey you can't travel without baggage. Everyone has baggage *(as he sets his boxes marked "Status" and "Quo" down so they are clearly visible)*, even missionaries have baggage, and I've got mine.

(looks at the couple seated behind the barrier and says to the audience) We must reach these people. They are so needy. Look at them, these dear people are so hungry for the truth. What they need is someone to go to them with a proven methodology, with our tried and true separatist, fundamentalist *tradition.* What we need is someone who believes in the Great Commission where it says "Go into all the world and *do church.*" I can just see those natives now in the pews, the organ on the right, the piano on the left. Ah, that's glory. Let's get them in church. I have a vision to see this church filled. We'll have our welcome committee, our ushers taking offerings, GLORY! I'm going to reach these folks for Christ! *(takes a drink of water)*

(The MISSIONARY approaches the barrier again. This time he calls out to the couple, "Come to church," and begins singing, "Onward Christian Soldiers." The couple pays no attention, so he now sings "Bringing In the Sheaves.")

MISSIONARY: *(pleading)* Ah, come on in to church, sheaves.

(The couple yawns.)

MISSIONARY: These folks are not as hungry and receptive as I thought they were. Maybe I should try my tract ministry. That will overcome the barrier that separates them from us.

(The MISSIONARY returns to the barrier. Taking a handful of "tracts," he throws them across the barrier at the couple and waits

for a response. They do not respond, so he returns to the audience.)

MISSIONARY: What a lack of respect. These pesky natives are arrogant. I can't believe they are that insensitive. They wouldn't even pick up my tracts and read them. But I'm not giving up. My preaching will get them. I'll just pull them off the streets with my preaching. I'm going out there to preach to them.

(The MISSIONARY faces the couple, standing so the audience can clearly hear and see, and begins to preach.)

MISSIONARY: I've come from America to tell you ignorant Europeans about God. You need to respond to that three entropic Person who came in the full duality of His nature and vicariously worked propitiation to give you that imparted righteousness, sanctification, and glorification whereby you may stand, accepted in the Beloved.

(They still don't respond. The European man blows his nose. The MISSIONARY, who is obviously distressed, faces the audience.)

MISSIONARY: You can't make it any clearer than that. These Europeans are pagans and dense. These ignorant savages won't listen. What we need is to get more people who will come here and help us do the job. What I need is more of me! *(he takes a drink of water)*

(The MISSIONARY faces the audience and speaks loudly.)

MISSIONARY: Is there anybody out there who will come and help me?

FIRST MISSIONARY RECRUIT: I want to help.

MISSIONARY: I warn you, these people are hard to reach and there are a lot of barriers. They won't even let you get to them.

FIRST MISSIONARY RECRUIT: *(bouncing a basketball as he comes)* I'm going to use sports to get around the barrier. I want

to get involved in their lives and community, and I hope
to make a contribution to their lives. This would put me in
constant contact with youth and their moms and dads. And
as we organize, I could even have contact with government
officials. In this way we could get to know and be known in
the community, always looking for a way to gain a hearing
for the gospel. I get excited when I think that maybe God
can use my sports and organizational skills to bring people
to Him.

Maybe I could invite professional athletes who are
Christians to come and help train the kids, and then have
special occasions where we could share Christ with them.

(He goes around the barrier and stands beside the couple.)

MISSIONARY: That doesn't sound like real missionary work to
me. You start throwing a ball around and you could hit my
baggage and upset the STATUS QUO. Is there anyone else
who would help me?

SECOND MISSIONARY RECRUIT: *(carrying a quilt in her hand)*
I would like to get around the barrier by using my skills
in crafts. Perhaps we could open a family and youth center
where the women could come and have a place to do their
crafts. I understand that in some countries, homes are very
crowded and there are not a lot of places for people to get
together. Perhaps we could open our building and could
teach crafts. This way we could build relationships and make
a contribution to their lives. This would provide an excellent
setting for sharing Christ with people who otherwise
wouldn't hear. I'm going to use my creative skills to try
to get around the barriers.

*(She walks around the barrier and goes and stands beside the
couple.)*

MISSIONARY: *(looking disgusted)* Anyone else?

THIRD MISSIONARY RECRUIT: *(carrying a briefcase)* I'd like to use my business skills to get around the barriers so that men can hear about the Lord Jesus Christ. I understand that in some countries men spend so much time on the job that it's difficult to find time to build relationships, win them to Christ, and disciple them. My idea would be to form an organization that would offer seminars for businessmen to teach them about strategic planning, goal setting, and problem solving. Those are the skills I know. I understand many companies are looking for help in this area. Many companies conduct their training sessions in English, so perhaps we could tap into some of our friends in America who have special expertise to come on special assignments. There are men of prestige who love the Lord. Maybe they could come and help us get into the business community, where we would have a good opportunity to build relationships with men and win them to Christ. I'm going to use my business skills to reach men for Christ. *(he goes around the barrier and stands next to the couple)*

MISSIONARY: *(by now quite disgusted)* NEXT.

LAST RECRUIT: *(enter the* LAST RECRUIT, *bringing a guitar)* I'm going to use music, the universal language, to get past the barriers.

MISSIONARY: Oh that won't work. I've tried that; they don't like good music. *(picks up glass and drinks)*

LAST RECRUIT: I'm going to use my music and drama skills to speak to people in a way they understand. As the church is formed, I have a vision to develop a dynamic, heartfelt worship. We are commanded to love God with "all our heart and all our soul and all our mind and all our strength."

MISSIONARY: Hey, wait a minute. Where's your piano; where's your organ? How can you do church with a guitar? Why don't you use the instruments of the piano and the organ, just like in the Bible? *(starts drinking water)*

LAST RECRUIT: *(reading from the Bible)* Psalm 150 says that
stringed instruments, like the guitar, are used in the Bible
in the praise of God. We read "Praise God in the sanctuary,
praise Him in His mighty heavens, praise Him for His acts
of power, praise Him for His surpassing greatness, praise
Him with the sounding of the trumpet, praise Him with
the harp and lyre. (The lyre is a stringed instrument like
a guitar, you know.) Praise Him with the tambourine and
dancing."

(At the word dancing, the MISSIONARY *begins to choke, and spits
out the water he is drinking.)*

MISSIONARY: What version is that?

LAST RECRUIT: *(continues to read)* "Praise Him with the strings
and flute, praise Him with the clash of cymbals, praise Him
with the sounding cymbals, let everything that has breath
praise the Lord. Praise the Lord." I want to reach Europeans
through music. *(he goes and stands by the couple)*

MISSIONARY: *(turning to the audience and muttering to himself)*
Where are the real missionaries who want to do church?

*(He walks over to his two boxes. As he picks up "STATUS" and
"QUO," he looks at them, then speaks.)*

MISSIONARY: We may not have crossed the barriers but at least
we kept the faith.

CHILDREN'S DRAMAS

by Iris Gray Dowling

Four exciting short plays for use by actors, with puppets, or as readings. These dramatic missions sketches are especially suitable for children ages 8–12.

Iris Gray Dowling is a freelance writer who has spent more than 35 years as an educator and director of children's church. Mrs. Dowling has published over 500 poems, plays, and articles for use in church ministries. Her desire is to inspire young people to wholly commit themselves to the Lord.

THE TURNING POINT

Characters:
> STEVE: a Christian boy
> BRYAN: neighborhood friend who listens
>> *(can use a girl for this part)*
> ROBIN: boy who doesn't want to listen
>> *(can use a girl for this part)*

Pronunciation Key:
> *Auca* (rhyme cow-ow-ka)
> *Quichua* (keech-wa)
> *Dayuma* (dye-u-ma)
> *Curaray* (coo-ra-rye)

AT RISE: STEVE *is in the yard reading.*

*(*BRYAN *and* ROBIN *enter Stage Right.)*

STEVE: Hi, Bryan. Hi, Robin.

BRYAN: What you been doing? We missed you.

STEVE: My church is having a missions' conference.

ROBIN: Oh, that's why I haven't seen you.

BRYAN: Didn't you want to play on the ball team? Now it's too late to sign up.

STEVE: That's all right. I've learned lots of interesting things about five missionaries who tried to reach a tribe of savage Indians in Ecuador, South America.

ROBIN: I didn't know there were savage Indians, today.

STEVE: It's not exactly today. This story happened in 1956.

ROBIN: Must've been a big tribe to have five missionary families there.

STEVE: The missionaries worked with different tribes in Ecuador. Some missionaries went into jungle areas to study tribal languages. After they had learned the language, other missionaries stayed to teach people about God's love and put the Bible into their own language.

ROBIN: They don't still kill people now, do they?

STEVE: No, that's an interesting part of this story.

BRYAN: What changed them?

STEVE: It's a long story, but it's exciting if you want me to tell you.

BRYAN: Well, hurry up and tell us.

ROBIN: *(turns to walk away)* You can listen if you want to, Bryan, but I've got more to do than sit around and talk about some savages in some country or other.

STEVE: It all started when God sent two missionaries, Jim Elliot and Pete Fleming, to the Quichua Indians in Ecuador. The Quichuas feared another tribe called the Aucas.

ROBIN: *(turns back)* The Quichuas, huh?

BRYAN: You mean one tribe of Indians were afraid of other Indians?

STEVE: Aucas were known as killers, even spearing some in their own tribe.

ROBIN: How can they prove that?

STEVE: Dayuma, a frightened Auca girl, escaped and came to the Quichua tribe.

BRYAN: Did she speak the same language?

STEVE: No, but Jim Elliot worked on translating the Quichua language.

BRYAN: How did he understand this Auca girl?

STEVE: I'm not sure. I guess the missionaries sensed she was afraid. She stayed with the Quichuas, and the missionaries learned enough words to figure out her story.

BRYAN: Go on. Those Auca people really sound scary.

STEVE: They didn't know much about people outside their own tribe. They spoke an unwritten language. They killed people to protect their village, and for other reasons besides.

ROBIN: I don't blame them for protecting themselves.

BRYAN: Did these missionary men try to hurt them?

STEVE: No, but no one knows what the Aucas thought. Killing was their way of life.

BRYAN: Why would missionaries bother with such killers?

STEVE: Jim Elliot and four other mission families felt God wanted them to tell the Aucas the message of His love.

BRYAN: That seems like a dangerous thought, wouldn't you say?

ROBIN: I don't know why this Jim guy would want to waste his life on a few savage Indians.

STEVE: He knew people everywhere need to hear about God's love. Jim Elliot said, "Who will tell them if I don't? I'm ready to die for their salvation, if I have to."

ROBIN: But he couldn't even speak their language.

STEVE: You're getting ahead of me. But you're right.

ROBIN: I bet he learned from Dayuma.

STEVE: You guessed it. With his special language training, he listened to the sounds of her words and wrote them down.

BRYAN: That sounds like a humongous job.

STEVE: That's where his special training helped. He felt so strongly that he had to tell people about Jesus. He prayed as he worked on the words and sounds of the Auca language.

ROBIN: I can't believe God wants people to go places where they might get killed.

STEVE: These five men and their wives prayed a long time before attempting to contact the Aucas. They learned words for "I like you," and "I want to be your friend."

ROBIN: And they expected the Aucas to accept them immediately? Seems like they're walking right into a death trap.

STEVE: No, they didn't move that fast. The men flew a plane

over the Auca village once a week and yelled out the
friendly words.

ROBIN: Those Indians must have been scared. Did they know
what a plane was?

STEVE: Maybe not at first. But later they came out of the
jungle each time they saw the plane and took the gifts
the missionaries dropped.

ROBIN: Oh! How long did that go on?

STEVE: About six weeks, then the Aucas put a feathered
headband on the plane's gift line.

BRYAN: Got friendly, huh? Did the missionaries decide to land?

STEVE: Not right away. All the missionary families prayed for
13 more weeks. Then they expected success in reaching the
Aucas.

BRYAN: Did the men continue flying over with gifts?

STEVE: Yeah, the families prayed a lot more and spent time
preparing. When they felt the Aucas were ready, they hunted
for a landing place along the Curaray River.

BRYAN: This is getting exciting!

STEVE: They landed and made a camp, which they named Palm
Beach.

BRYAN: And the Indians came.

STEVE: The men didn't see anyone for a few days.

BRYAN: Oooh! This is getting scary!

STEVE: Then the Indians came and ate lunch with them.

BRYAN: Pheew! What a relief!

STEVE: Then the Aucas left. And the men prayed they'd come
back and bring more of their people. They called their
wives by shortwave radio to report all was going well.
They promised to call back at 4:30.

BRYAN: That's a good story.

ROBIN: I don't see anything exciting about it.

STEVE: But that's not the end. The men didn't call their wives
at 4:30.

BRYAN: Why?

STEVE: The Aucas came back and killed them with spears.

ROBIN: How did their wives find out?

BRYAN: I hope they didn't get killed looking for them.

STEVE: No, a search party was sent in. But that's not the end either. Something better happened later.

ROBIN: It's got to be better. This part is gruesome. Why would God let good men die when they're working for Him?

STEVE: Because the whole world heard this story.

ROBIN: What do you mean? Didn't this all happen way back in the jungle?

STEVE: Remember, they had short wave radios. Magazines and newspapers got the story and printed it all over the world.

BRYAN: How could that have an effect on the Aucas when they couldn't read?

STEVE: It affected Christians all over the world. They started praying for the salvation of the Aucas.

ROBIN: Their prayers helped?

STEVE: Prayer is powerful. Prayer breaks Satan's power over people and helps missionaries do God's work in a better way.

BRYAN: Does prayer work like that in our country, too?

STEVE: Sure, if Christians would pray more, we'd be amazed what God would do.

BRYAN: I still can't understand God letting those men die.

STEVE: It's hard for us to understand God's ways. He doesn't think the way we do. He sees everything in the light of eternal values.

ROBIN: Are you saying God was pleased with those Aucas who killed the missionaries?

STEVE: No. God wasn't pleased with their sin of murder, just like He's not pleased with any of our sins.

BRYAN: So, will those murderers go to heaven?

STEVE: If they confessed their sins to God and asked for His forgiveness, yes they will go to heaven!

BRYAN: Did any of them do that?

STEVE: Here's the real turning point of the story. Dayuma went back to the Aucas and told them she had asked Jesus to forgive her sins. She told them Jesus loved them, too. Another turning point came when the Aucas invited Jim's wife, Elisabeth, to come and teach them about God's love and forgiveness. Mrs. Elliot and her baby daughter lived right with the Aucas.

ROBIN: What a scary thing for her to do!

STEVE: You're right, but Elisabeth Elliot learned enough language from Dayuma to teach them of Jesus' love. After a while, the same men who killed her husband accepted Jesus as their Savior from sins.

BRYAN: That is a strange turn of events!

STEVE: That's still not all. Eventually the whole village believed and accepted Jesus as Savior.

BRYAN: I guess the Acuas could see Mrs. Elliot forgave them when she came to live with them.

ROBIN: I don't know how she could forgive them.

STEVE: She forgave them just as God forgave her.

ROBIN: Why did God need to forgive her? What awful things had she done?

STEVE: The Bible says we all are sinners. We all need God's forgiveness from our sins.

ROBIN: Are you saying I am a sinner? I need forgiveness from sin?

STEVE: Yes, Jim Elliot accepted God's forgiveness for his sins when he was a young boy. I did, too. That's why getting on the ball team doesn't matter so much. What God wants is more important than anything else!

BRYAN: You sure gave us a lot to think about, Steve.

ROBIN: I've heard enough of this gory story. I'm going to play ball now. Are you coming, Bryan? *(walks off Stage Right)*

STEVE: Why don't you guys come to the missionary conference with me tonight? We'll hear more true stories of how God's love changes people's lives.

BRYAN: I'll ask my parents and give you a call.

STEVE: Okay, Bryan. See you later. *(EXITS Stage Left)*

(BRYAN *EXITS Stage Right)*

INVISIBLE REWARDS

*The Woods children don't want to share their home with visiting
missionaries during a missions conference. Their parents plan to
do so anyway, and the children learn the rewards of sharing and
having friends who serve the Lord.*

Characters:
DAD
MOM
AMY WOODS: child
JOEL WOODS: child
MELISSA WOODS: child
MR. AND MRS. ANDERS: missionaries

SCENE ONE

*At the Woods' home the day before their church missions conference.
The Woods children are having cookies and milk. They argue about
who will give up their room for the Anders, a visiting missionary
couple.*

AMY: I think you should give up your room, since you have
your room to yourself.
MELISSA: Yeah, Joel. That way you're the only one who has to
give up a bed.
MOM: *(enters carrying broom, mops, dust cloths, and vacuum)* What
are you kids arguing about?
JOEL: But my bed isn't a big queen- or king-sized one.

77

MELISSA: They probably don't have a big bed where they come from anyway.

MOM: Children, I can't believe this selfishness. Shouldn't we be glad to share our home with people who serve the Lord in a faraway place?

JOEL: Why do they have to sleep at our house?

AMY: Lots of other families in our church could take them.

MOM: Dad and I want you to get better acquainted with the missionaries our church supports.

AMY: But you didn't ask us.

MELISSA: I don't see why you want us to learn about missionaries now.

MOM: This missions conference is a perfect opportunity for you to get to know them. *(firmly)* Now let's get busy and clean the house. I expect you each to clean a room. Take your pick, or I'll choose it for you. *(MOM has mops and a broom in her hand.)*

AMY: *(takes mop)* I guess I'll take the kitchen.

JOEL: *(gets dust mop)* I'll take the family room.

MELISSA: *(gets vacuum cleaner)* I suppose I'll take our bedroom.

MOM: Good, you can all get started now.

(All exit stage to clean the rooms.)

SCENE TWO

At the Woods' home on the first day of the missions conference, the Woods arrive home from church early and are discussing the missionaries visit.

MOM: I'm glad we got home from church before the Anders came.

DAD: I know. I need to straighten up my study. Mr. Anders might want to use it before the next service.

AMY: Why does he need your study? We gave them our room.

DAD: It's quiet for him to study and pray.

JOEL: What about you? Don't you need it too, Dad?

DAD: Yes, but I can share for a few days.

MOM: It's good someone in this house is willing to share his room.

MELISSA: Mom, you're not the one who has to sleep on the floor.

MOM: God likes to reward those who have a good attitude about sharing.

MELISSA: I wonder what kind of a reward He'll give me.

MOM: God wants a willing heart and a cheerful giver.

MELISSA: I thought a cheerful giver meant giving money.

DAD: Not always. I'm sure it means anything you have to give to the Lord.

MELISSA: Even my room?

AMY: Even my bed?

DAD: Yes, all of that. Giving cheerfully makes God happy. *(pause)* He sometimes gives His rewards later.

AMY: I'd like to have mine right now.

MELISSA: Me, too.

MOM: Please, kids, try not to argue so much.

DAD: Your Mom's right. Try to make the Anders' visit pleasant.

ALL KIDS: Okay, Dad.

DAD: Good. *(pause)* Here they come. *(knock is heard)*

MOM: *(opens door)* Hello. Come in. Welcome to our home.

DAD: Melissa will show you to your room. You can leave your bags here for now.

MOM: Let's have lunch, then you can unpack.

DAD: Our house is your home while you're here. Please make yourselves comfortable.

MOM: *(motions for MR. AND MRS. ANDERS to sit at table; carries dishes to table)* Come sit down. Lunch is ready.

MR. ANDERS: May I ask the blessing?

DAD: Certainly. *(pause)* Let's all pray. *(all bow heads)*

MR. ANDERS: Dear Heavenly Father, thank you for this family who so graciously gave us a home for a few days. Reward them for their kindness. Bless them and their children. Bless this food to our bodies. Give us strength to serve you better. Amen.

JOEL: *(to* MR. ANDERS*)* Where do you work as a missionary?

MR. ANDERS: In Brazil.

JOEL: Why did you want to go to Brazil?

MR. ANDERS: The Lord wanted me to go tell others about God's love and salvation. I had a successful business here at home; then God called me to be a missionary.

JOEL: Do you make as much money now?

MR. ANDERS: No, but money isn't the most important thing. I wanted to obey God.

MRS. ANDERS: You know God's blessings and rewards will last into eternity.

JOEL: Won't you have to wait a long time for that?

MR. ANDERS: Maybe . . . but it's more satisfying to know we're doing what God wants us to do.

JOEL: I guess you're right.

MR. ANDERS: You see, God calls everyone who is a believer in Jesus Christ to be a missionary. God uses some people right here at home, and others He sends to various places around the world.

JOEL: You mean my dad is a missionary, too?

MR. ANDERS: Any Christian is a missionary. Your dad has an important part in sending us to Brazil.

JOEL: My dad helps send you to Brazil?

MR. ANDERS: Sure. He's part of our missionary team. He works here and we work in Brazil. But God rewards us both according to how we share in the work.

JOEL: I didn't know it worked that way.

AMY: What about Mom?

MR. ANDERS: She's part of the team, too.

AMY: How?

MR. ANDERS: She helps your father keep the house running smoothly so he can concentrate on his business.

AMY: I never thought of it that way.

MELISSA: Sometimes we don't make it very easy for her.

AMY: What about your wife? What does she do?

MR. ANDERS: I'll let her tell you about her work.

MRS. ANDERS: Now that our children are in college, I can be involved in the work.

AMY: You have children in college?

MELISSA: How can you afford it?

MRS. ANDERS: God provided scholarships for them. That's one of our rewards.

AMY: You got a reward?

MRS. ANDERS: Yes, and I do the same things your mother does. I cook, wash clothes, sew, and clean. I teach a women's Bible study, and a children's Bible club after school during the week.

AMY: What do you do on Sunday?

MRS. ANDERS: I teach Sunday school and tell stories to children during church.

AMY: You do a lot of teaching.

MELISSA: Did you study to be a teacher?

MRS. ANDERS: Yes, I did. I always wanted to teach.

MELISSA: Did you ever teach school?

MRS. ANDERS: I taught in the United States while my husband finished college.

MELISSA: Why did you stop?

MRS. ANDERS: We had our first baby.

AMY: Did you teach after that?

MRS. ANDERS: I taught Sunday school. Then I home-schooled our children when we lived in Brazil.

AMY: Boy, you never stopped teaching, did you?

MRS. ANDERS: No, I love teaching. And the Lord gave me
  a lot to do.

MR. ANDERS: You see, when we are willing, God uses our
  talents for His purpose.

AMY: You make it sound so easy. Don't you get tired sometimes?

MRS. ANDERS: Yes, I do, just like anybody else. But the Lord
  gives strength when I need it.

MR. ANDERS: Well that's enough "job talk." How about playing
  a game? Joel do you play chess?

JOEL: Sure do! I'll go get it. *(exits; pauses; returns with the game;*
  JOEL *and* MR. ANDERS *play)*

ANNOUNCER: Joel and Mr. Anders enjoy playing chess from
  time to time over the next two days. The girls enjoy
  listening to Mrs. Anders tell stories about missionary life
  in Brazil.

SCENE THREE

*Two days later at the Woods' home, the Anders are preparing to
leave. The children help carry luggage to the door.*

JOEL: Mr. Anders, I wish you didn't have to leave.

MR. ANDERS: We have other churches and friends to visit
  before going back to Brazil.

JOEL: Can you come visit us again?

MR. ANDERS: Maybe. When we do, I'll be ready for a challenge
  from you in that chess game.

JOEL: I'm going to practice so I'll win.

MR. ANDERS: Good! I can't wait!

AMY: Mrs. Anders, thanks for telling us stories about the boys
  and girls of Brazil.

MELISSA: Yes, Mrs. Anders. We'll never forget your stories.
  Please tell us more when you come back.

MRS. ANDERS: I'll be glad to. Maybe I can bring my children next time.

AMY: Oh, would you please?

MRS. ANDERS: *(hugs them)* Goodbye, Amy. 'Bye Melissa.

AMY and MELISSA: We'll write to you in Brazil.

MRS. ANDERS: That will mean so much to me. I love to get e-mail and letters from my friends back home.

CHILDREN: We'll pray for you, too.

MR. ANDERS: That's really important to us.

MRS. ANDERS: Thanks for everything. Thank you, girls, for sharing your room. The Lord will reward you.

AMY and MELISSA: He already has. *(everyone waves goodbye as MOM and DAD glance at each other and smile; then smile at the kids; all exit the stage)*

WHOM SHALL I SEND?

Two missionary kids talk with their friends about missionaries and their work just before leaving with their family for missionary service in a foreign country.

Characters:
BECKY: a missionary kid (MK)
JOSH: MK and Becky's younger brother
BRIAN: a friend
LESLEY: a friend

Setting:
Takes place in a contemporary room of a home

AT RISE: BECKY and JOSH are cleaning out boxes in the family room.

(BRIAN knocks and enters Stage Left.)

JOSH: Hi, Brian. *(JOSH turns to go with BRIAN)*
BECKY: Hi, Brian. Josh, did you finish cleaning your room? Have you decided what you'll take with you?
JOSH: I tried, but I'm having a hard time deciding what to take and what to leave.
BECKY: Okay. I'll help you tonight. Lesley's coming over soon. Let's just play with our friends this afternoon.
BRIAN: It must be hard to be a missionary.
BECKY: Especially to get ready to go as a foreign missionary.
BRIAN: Foreign missionary? What does that mean?

BECKY: That means we live outside North America.

BRIAN: Can you be a missionary if you stay here in America?

BECKY: Sure, there are many missionaries in the United States and Canada.

BRIAN: I didn't know North Americans needed missionaries.

BECKY: Lots of people here don't know much about Jesus.

JOSH: Some people feel they don't need Jesus. They don't even go to church.

BECKY: That's why some missionaries in the United States and Canada are called church planters.

BRIAN: Oh . . . you mean they dig a gigantic hole in the ground and plant a church, then push the soil around it?

BECKY: No . . . I'm not joking! They start new churches.

BRIAN: *(laughing)* Isn't that what I said? They plant a church.

JOSH: *(sighing)* Church planters go where people need to learn about Jesus.

BECKY: They start a Bible study group that grows into a bigger group and, one day, that group becomes a church.

JOSH: Then the people plan how they'll get a building for their church.

BECKY: You see, Brian, the building doesn't make the church, the people do!

BRIAN: Oh . . . I see.

(KNOCK is heard; BECKY *answers door;* LESLEY *enters Stage Right.)*

BECKY: Come in, Lesley.

BRIAN: Tell me, Josh, why do you need to go to _____? *(insert the name of the country of your choice; if possible choose a country where a radio ministry is part of the missionary's work)*

JOSH: My Mom and Dad are going where God called them and where they can do their best work for Him.

BRIAN: Can't they tell people about Jesus anywhere?

JOSH: Of course, but our Dad is an electrical engineer.

BECKY: His kind of work is needed at radio stations.

LESLEY: I know . . . he's a radio preacher.

BECKY: No, he's not the preacher, but he tells others about Jesus just like he does here.

BRIAN: How does an electrical engineer tell people about Jesus?

BECKY: He mostly works on radio and electrical equipment so the messages can get out over the airwaves.

JOSH: He makes sure the broadcasting equipment is working so the gospel message can go out over thousands of miles.

BRIAN: You mean he talks over the radio?

JOSH: *(shakes head)* No . . . he fixes them!

BRIAN: I know, I was just joking.

LESLEY: *(lifts eyebrows)* Fixing radios? That's being a missionary?

BECKY: Sure! Not all missionaries preach and teach. Some help preachers get the gospel message to people who've never heard it. They also work in their missionary church, just as they would here at home.

LESLEY: Sounds exciting anyway.

BECKY: Today missionaries need to be trained to do lots more than just preach.

LESLEY: Really . . . like what?

BECKY: Doctors, nurses, teachers, artists, and writers . . .

JOSH: Pilots, engineers, computer operators, and accountants.

BRIAN: You mean my Dad could be a missionary?

BECKY: If God wants him to.

JOSH: First, a missionary has to know Jesus as His Savior, then be willing to tell others about Jesus wherever He wants them to.

BRIAN: *(thinking gesture)* But my Dad doesn't do any of those jobs you just named.

JOSH: If God calls him and he's willing, God would find the place to use him.

BECKY: You see, God sends people where He can use their talents best.

BRIAN: Oh . . . you mean whatever my Dad can do, God could use it?

BECKY: Just like He's using my Dad—not as a preacher—but as an electrical engineer to help preachers get the message to more people.

BRIAN: I wish I could go with you.

BECKY: A very important part of our missionary team stays right here at home.

BRIAN: Your team?

BECKY: We need people like you to pray for us every day.

BRIAN: Is that all I have to do to be on your team?

JOSH: Yes, but we also need people at home to support us with money, or we can't go to the mission field.

BRIAN: You mean I can be a part of your mission team if I pray and give you money.

BECKY: Even if you can't give money . . . just pray.

BRIAN: Cool!

BECKY: God says in the Bible it's like farming: one person plants, another one waters the crop. They all receive an equal reward.

BRIAN: So the person who prays for you gets a reward the same as you do?

BECKY: You got it! God promises rewards to every faithful person on the mission team.

BRIAN: Awesome! You can be sure I'll pray for you. And I'll save some money to help you go.

LESLEY: Me, too.

JOSH: Thanks, Brian. Thanks, Lesley. You are our very special friends. We'll e-mail you and let you know what's happening.

BRIAN: Cool! I like getting mail.

LESLEY: Becky, would you write to me?

LESLEY: Let's go ride our bikes in the park while we're still close neighbors.

BECKY: It'll be easier for us to go away when we know you'll be praying for us.

OUR HOPE IS
IN THE LORD

Characters:

CHUNG: a Chinese Christian boy who has recently moved into the neighborhood

ALEX: a well-to-do American classmate

Setting:

On the street near their homes. Two classmates, Chung and Alex are on the way home after school.

CHUNG: Hi. How about coming over to my house to play ball?

ALEX: No-o-o, I can't.

CHUNG: Won't your mother let you?

ALEX: I don't know. I didn't ask.

CHUNG: Ask her if you can come tomorrow. I know my house isn't big, but we can play ball outside.

ALEX: You live in one of those apartments over there, don't you?

CHUNG: Yes, that's all we can afford right now. My mother cleans houses to earn enough money.

ALEX: Where's your dad?

CHUNG: He's in prison in China.

ALEX: Oh, is he a criminal or something?

CHUNG: No, he is not!

ALEX: Then why is he in prison?

CHUNG: You don't know what it's like to live in China, do you?

ALEX: What do you mean, like crowded?

CHUNG: It is crowded, but that's not what I meant. People who talk about Jesus are put in prison.

ALEX: Why did he do it, then?

CHUNG: Most Chinese leaders and many Chinese people are atheists.

ALEX: Atheists? Isn't that someone who doesn't believe in God?

CHUNG: Yes. Didn't you know communists are atheists?

ALEX: No, I don't know much about China. In fact, I don't know much about God either.

CHUNG: Don't you go to church?

ALEX: Not much.

CHUNG: I thought everyone in America goes to church.

ALEX: Not me. I never thought I needed to go to church. Most of my friends don't go either.

CHUNG: Would you go with me sometime?

ALEX: I don't know about that. *(pauses)* Tell me more about your dad.

CHUNG: My father is a very educated man. The government doesn't like intelligent, educated people. My father came from a very hard-working family.

ALEX: And they don't like that either?

CHUNG: You're right. We aren't allowed to have a Bible. When my father received the Lord Jesus as his Savior, he knew many people would never hear about Jesus if he didn't tell them.

ALEX: The government didn't like that either?

CHUNG: Right again. They followed my father, and watched him until they finally caught him talking about Jesus. They arrested him and put him in prison for four years.

ALEX: Then they let him out?

CHUNG: Yes, but they warned him never to talk about Jesus again.

ALEX: That wouldn't be too hard to obey, would it?

CHUNG: You don't know my father. He couldn't keep quiet

about the Lord Jesus Christ, who loved him and gave His life on the cross for him.

ALEX: Even when it meant going back to prison?

CHUNG: He knew millions of Chinese people had no way to hear about Jesus. And some who do believe are killed.

ALEX: Wow! I didn't know that. But I still don't see why your father risked his life.

CHUNG: He knew the people of China need hope—something to look forward to.

ALEX: What do you mean, hope?

CHUNG: If people know the Lord Jesus and receive Him as Savior, they know they will go to heaven. That's a much better place than anyone has ever known here on earth. Knowing they will go to heaven gives them hope.

ALEX: Nobody can know for sure if he's going to heaven. You have to be good, and give money to people, and lots of other stuff.

CHUNG: You're wrong there, Alex. We *can* know for sure that we're going to heaven. When we ask Jesus to forgive our sins and we receive Him as Savior, He does so much for us right now, and He also promises us a place in heaven. In fact, Jesus is preparing that place for us right now. The Bible calls that assurance of going to heaven "the blessed hope." We can look forward to that, no matter what wicked people do to us here on earth.

ALEX: You really believe that stuff, don't you?

CHUNG: Sure, my whole family does. Chinese people—and everyone else—need the hope that they can look forward to living in heaven.

ALEX: You still believe, even though this happened to your dad?

CHUNG: My father taught me to have hope in God because He will not fail us.

ALEX: How could your father still have hope when he's been put in prison?

CHUNG: Because he knows Jesus is with him. Even when he's beaten or has no food, God is with him, as He was with Elijah.

ALEX: Who's Elijah?

CHUNG: He was one of God's prophets written about in the Bible. When Elijah was all alone and hungry, God sent ravens to feed him.

ALEX: That's funny. God doesn't do that today.

CHUNG: Don't be too sure. You've never been hungry, have you?

ALEX: Not really. I can have whatever I want.

CHUNG: I know. (pauses) God can do anything for those who trust Him. Many times God has provided what my mother and I need.

ALEX: Where does your father sleep in the prison?

CHUNG: He certainly doesn't have a clean bed. His home right now is a small, dark cell with bugs and rats.

ALEX: And he wanted to talk about Jesus knowing he'd go back there?

CHUNG: My father knows that what happens to him here is not so important. The main thing in his mind is the people who have little or no way to hear about Jesus. They need to learn about heaven.

ALEX: But that heaven business is all in the future. He's suffering right now.

CHUNG: I know. The government watches him all the time. They want to send him away to a prison camp and give him the dirtiest, hardest work to do.

ALEX: Did they think he wouldn't do it?

CHUNG: Maybe, but my father knows how to work joyfully because he knows God is his real boss and won't let him suffer forever.

ALEX: Do you get any letters from him?

CHUNG: Only a few. He told us he now works in a sort of

sewer area. He told us to go to America if we got a chance. He'll come when God opens the way.

ALEX: He does seem hopeful. But what if he gets sick in that awful sewer place? You wouldn't even know whether he's sick or not.

CHUNG: My father knows God can do anything, even if it seems impossible to us. So he's willing to work in that sewer or go where God wants him, whether it's a prison camp or heaven.

ALEX: I'm glad you told me about your dad. I've never heard anything like this before.

CHUNG: I'm thankful for Christian people who helped us come to America. Many Chinese people try to get to America by promising to pay snakeheads.

ALEX: Collecting snakeheads doesn't sound like a very good job, either.

CHUNG: Oh, no. You don't understand. It's not really a job. We call crooked smugglers snakeheads. They make desperate Chinese pay thousands of dollars to get to America. It takes many years to pay them back.

ALEX: People really do that?

CHUNG: Sure they do. But I'm thankful we didn't have to come that way.

ALEX: So how did you get here?

CHUNG: American friends sent us money. Now we can go to church as often as we want.

ALEX: Oh, and you really go every week?

CHUNG: We go whenever church is open.

ALEX: Really?

CHUNG: Why don't you go with me this week?

ALEX: Maybe I will. I could stand some of your happiness. I have money and lots of things, but I don't have much hope for the future, and I'm not as happy as you are even now.

CHUNG: My faith and hope in Jesus make the difference.

ALEX: How can you be happy when your dad is being beaten and is in prison, and he didn't do anything wrong?

CHUNG: My father knows Jesus didn't deserve to be beaten and crucified on a cross for him. Jesus didn't do any wrong, either.

ALEX: I never thought about it that way.

CHUNG: There's so much to learn in the Bible. I'm so glad we can read our Bibles and go to church whenever we want to now.

ALEX: I don't know much about the Bible at all. How did you learn so much if you weren't allowed to read a Bible?

CHUNG: My father taught me when he was home. Then Mother taught me.

ALEX: I think I'd like to meet your mother.

CHUNG: You can meet her tomorrow if you come to my house.

ALEX: Okay, I'll ask my folks if I can come.

CHUNG: See you then. *(waves, leaves Stage Right)*

(ALEX leaves Stage Left)